EARLY TO MID-INTERMEDIATE

# PORTRAITS OF THE SKY

## 8 ORIGINAL PIANO SOLOS BY RANDALL HARTSELL

ISBN 978-1-4234-5714-5

WM
WILLIS MUSIC

Exclusively Distributed By

HAL•LEONARD®
CORPORATION
7777 W. BLUEMOUND RD. P.O. BOX 13819 MILWAUKEE, WI 53213

Visit Hal Leonard Online at
www.halleonard.com

# By the Moonlit Tides

Randall Hartsell

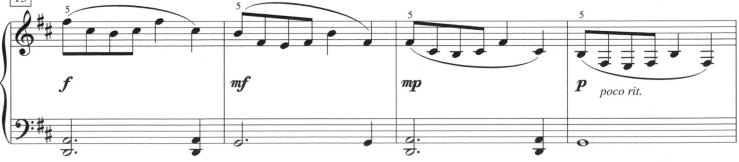

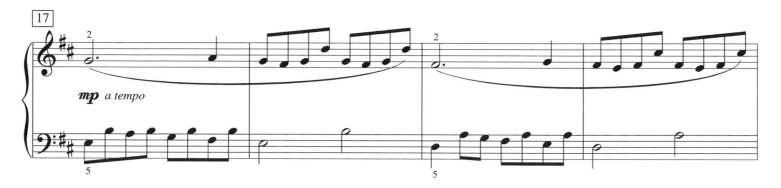

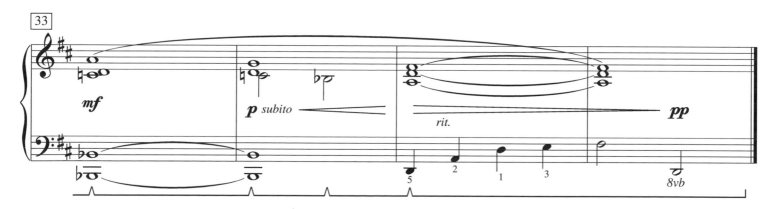

# Sunsets in Savannah

Randall Hartsell

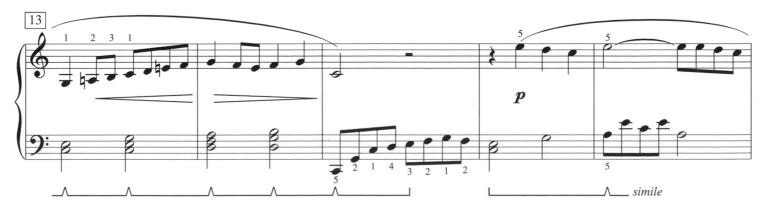

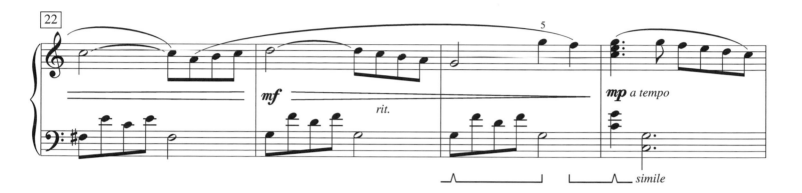

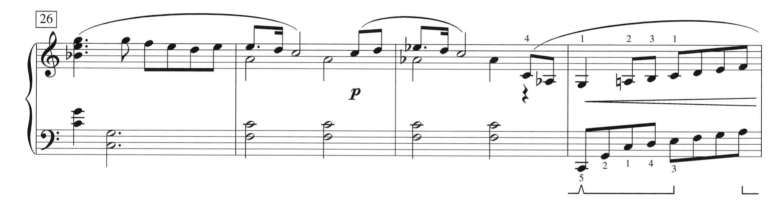

# Rainbow Falls

Randall Hartsell

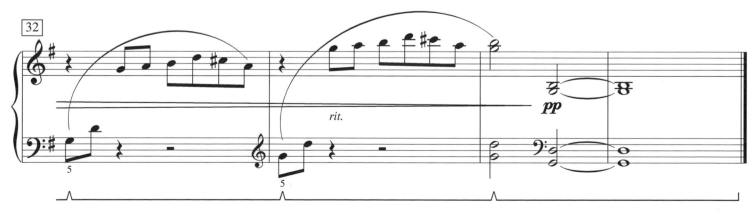

# Tomorrow's Rainbow

*for Linda Nelson*

Randall Hartsell

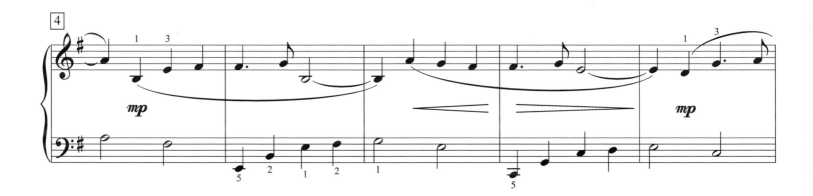

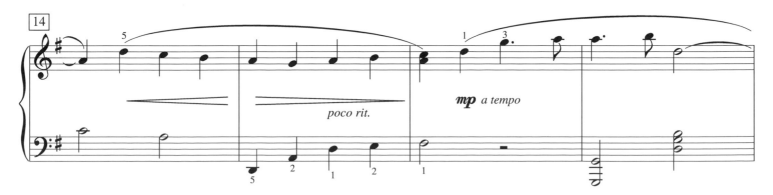

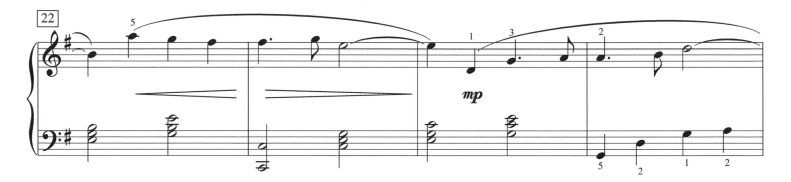

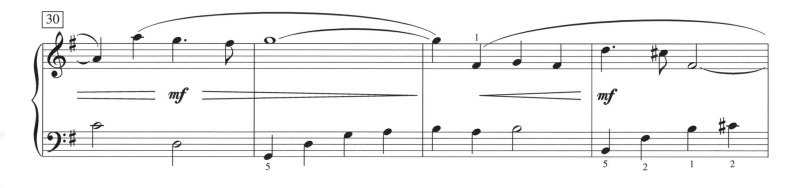

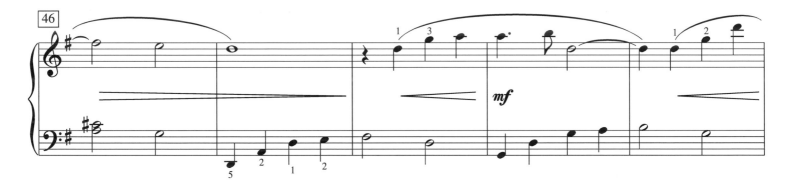

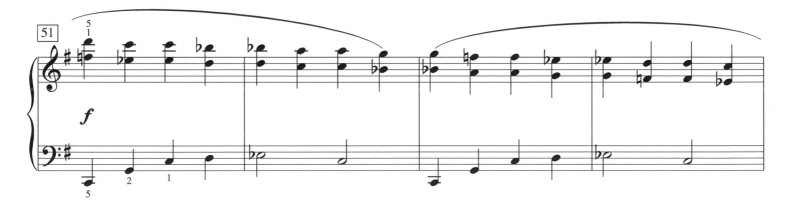

# Shimmering Stardust

Randall Hartsell

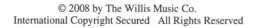

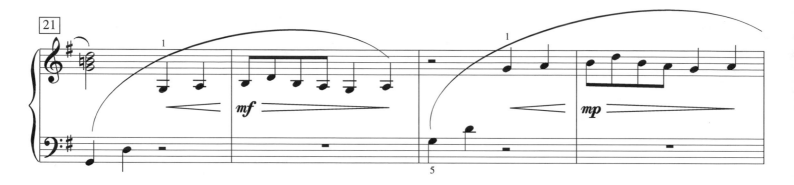

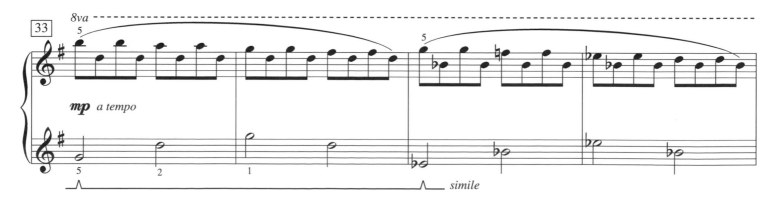

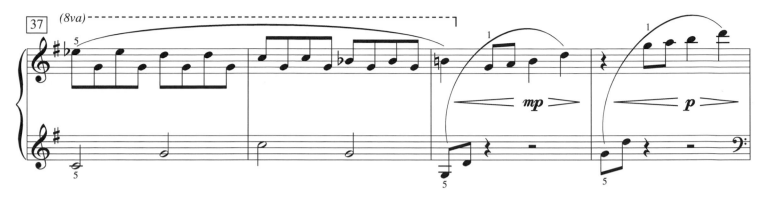

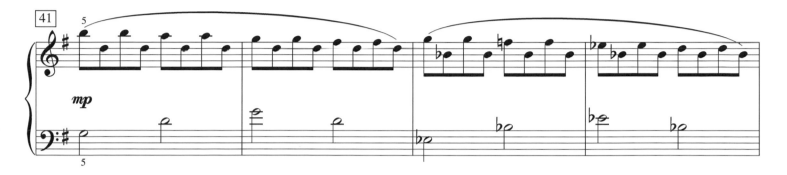

# Impressions in the Sky

Randall Hartsell

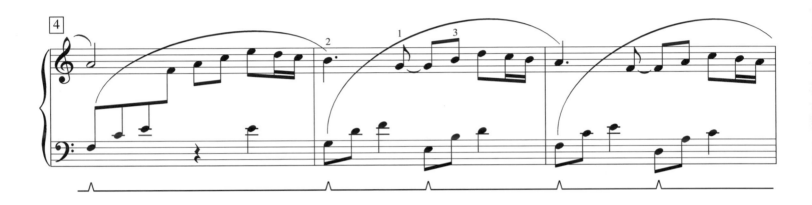

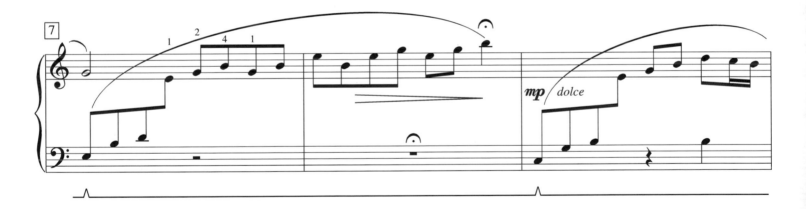

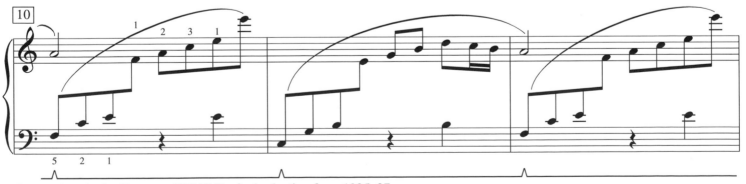

*Impressions in the Sky* was a NFMC Festival selection from 1995–97.

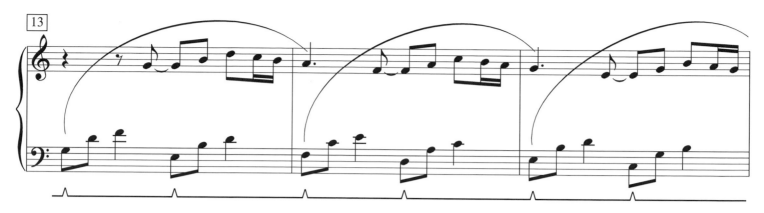

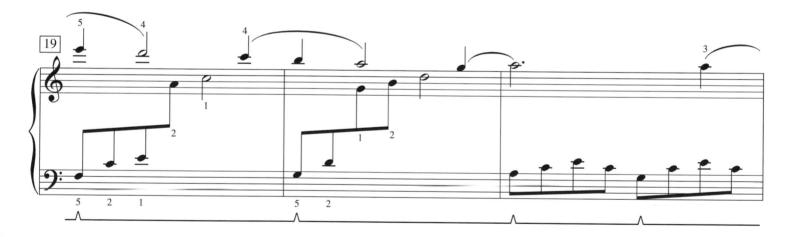

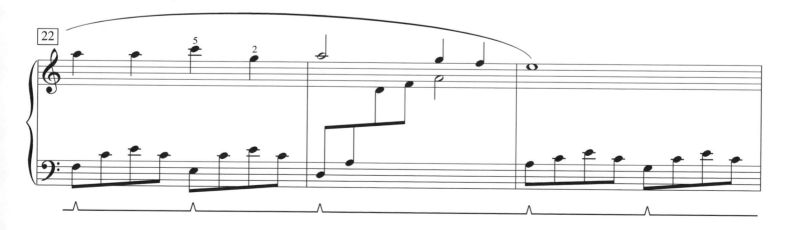

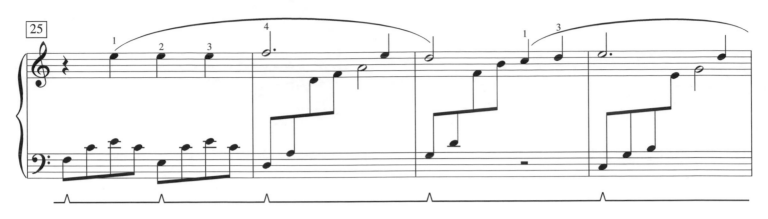

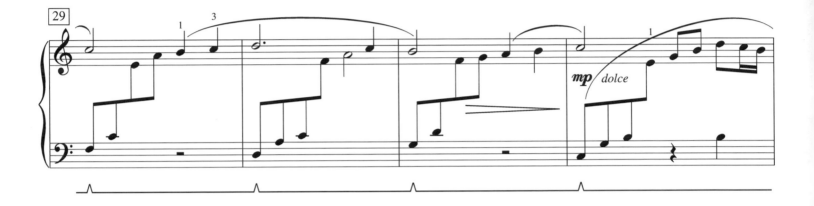

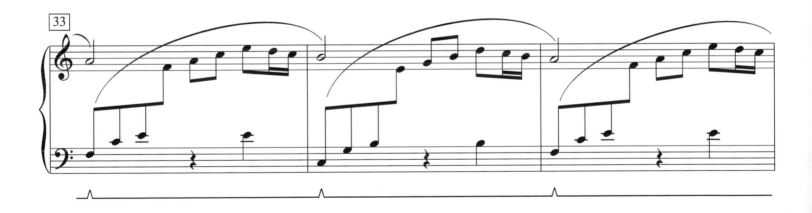

# September Sunset

*for Jewell Broadway*

Randall Hartsell

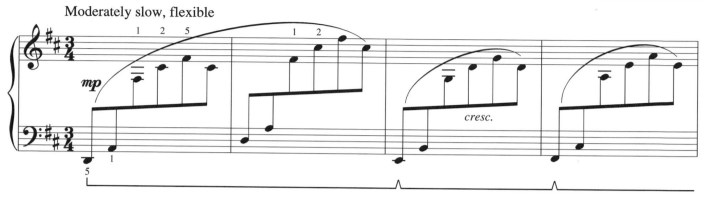

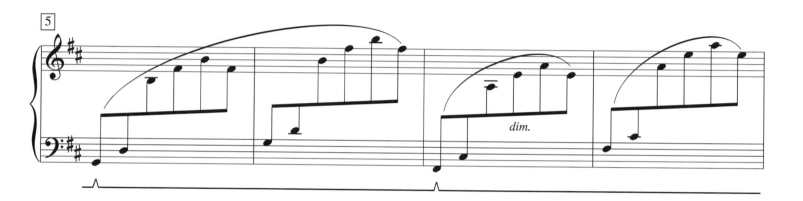

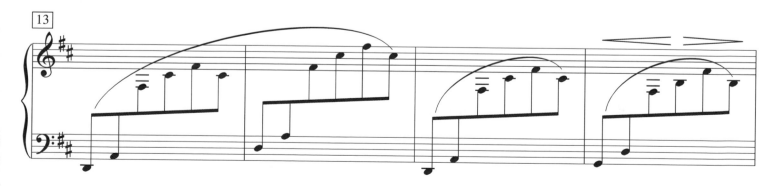

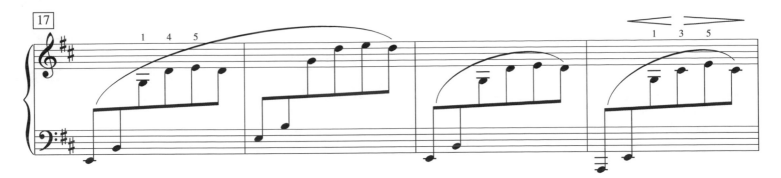

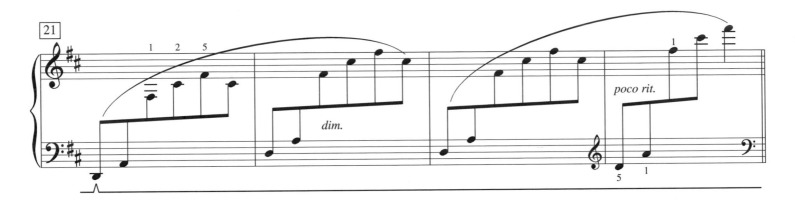

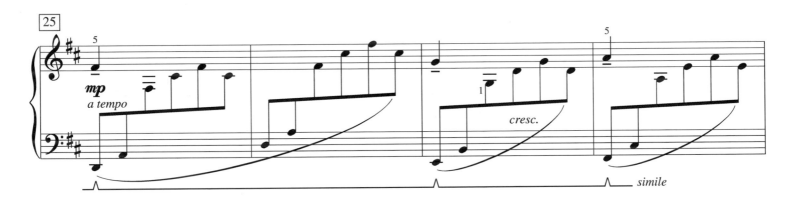

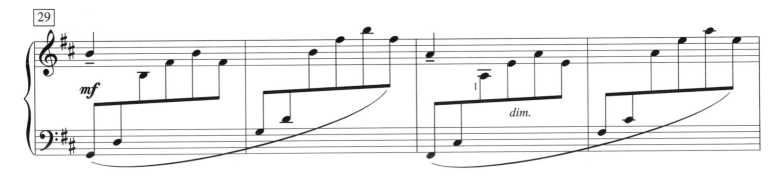

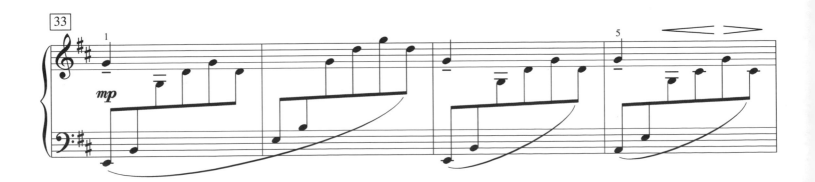

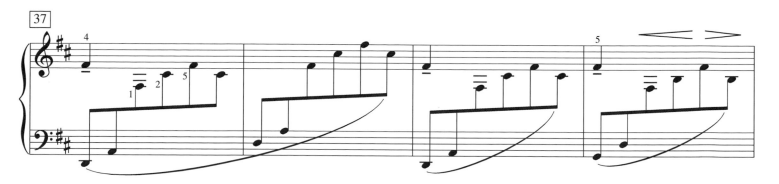

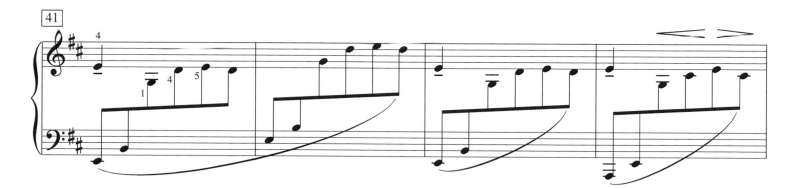

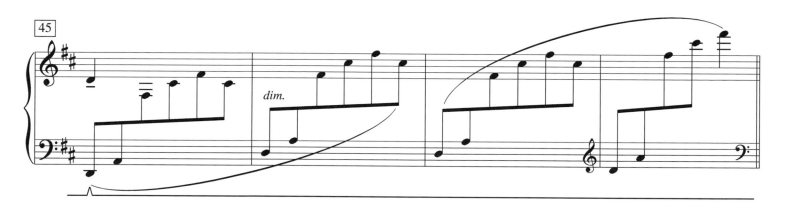

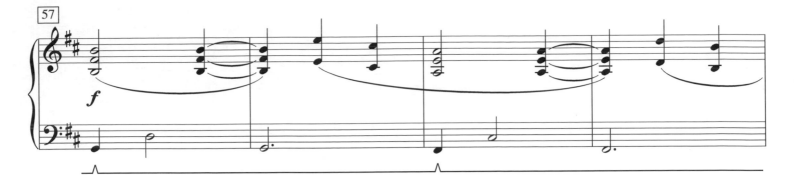

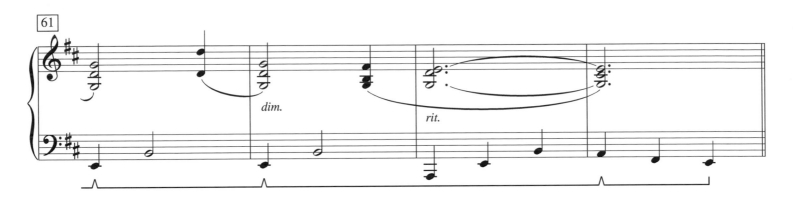

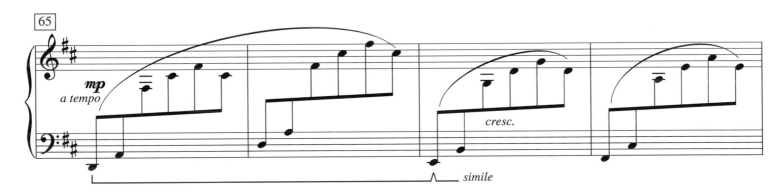

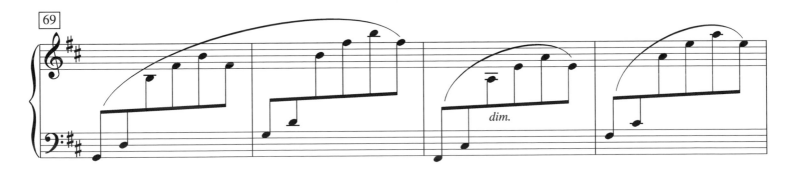

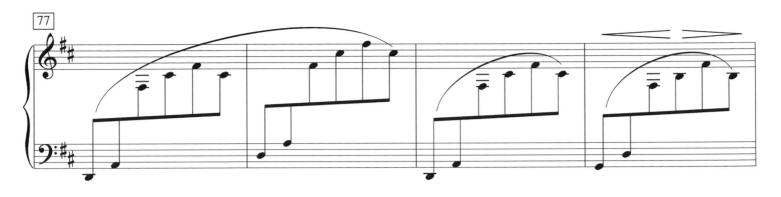

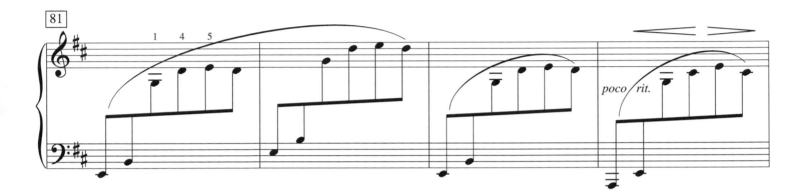

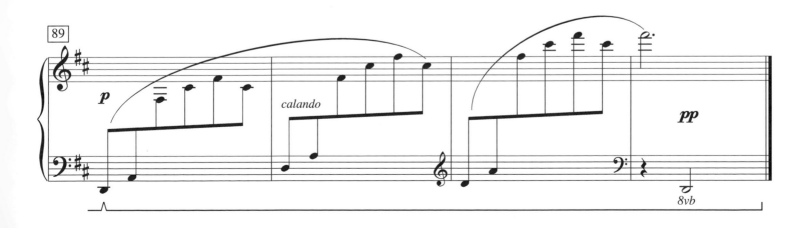

# Toward the Rising Sun

Randall Hartsell

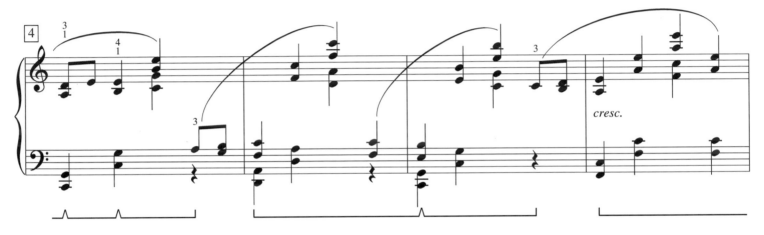

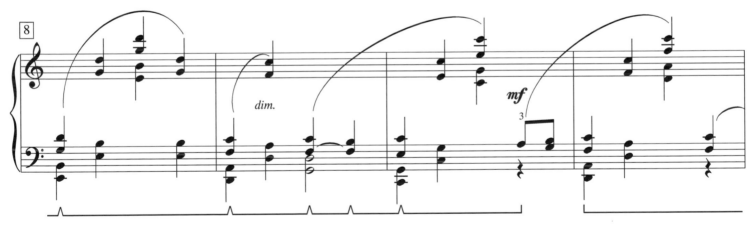

*Toward the Rising Sun* was a NFMC Festival selection from 1991–94.

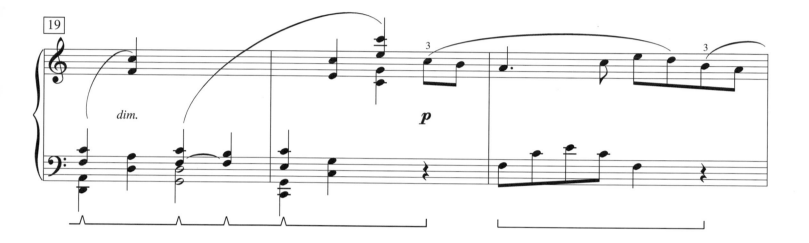

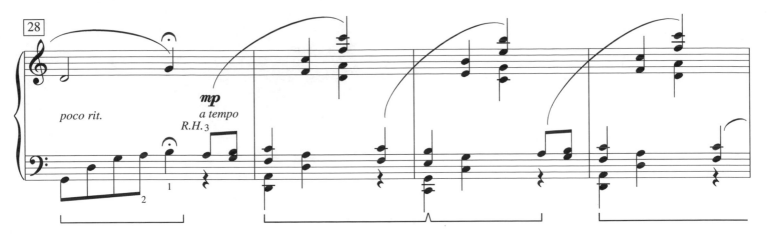

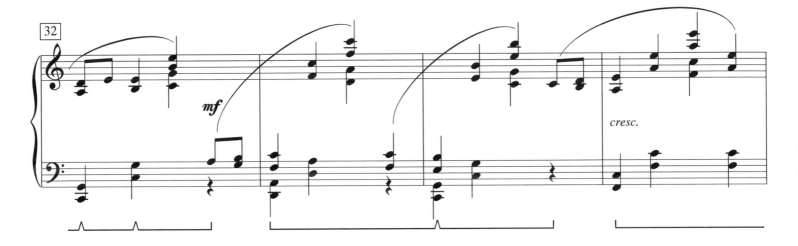

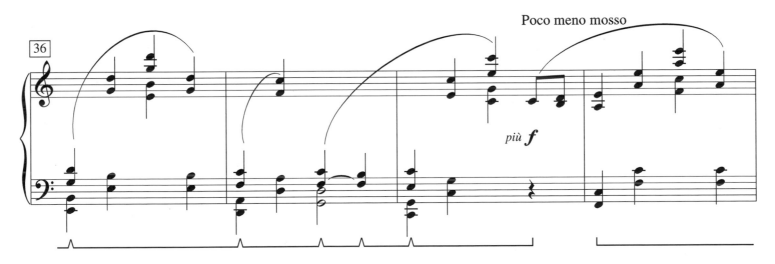